A Grace – Full Life

A GRACE-FULL LIFE

God's All-Reaching, Soul-Saving, Character-Shaping Never-Ending Love

A Grace-full Life

978-1-5018-3281-9
978-1-5018-3282-6 eBook

A Grace-Full Life: DVD

978-1-5018-3285-7

A Grace-Full Life: Leader Guide

978-1-5018-3283-3
978-1-5018-3284-0 eBook

Jorge Acevedo & Wes Olds

A GRACE-FULL LIFE

God's All-Reaching, Soul-Saving, Character-Shaping, Never-Ending Love

Leader Guide

Jenny Youngman, Contributor

Abingdon Press / Nashville

We dedicate this book to our two mothers,
Carmen Acevedo and Sandy Olds, who stand in
the rich heritage of Mary, the mother of Jesus.
Like Mary, our mothers have humbly lived
as servants of the Lord (Luke 1:38),
faithfully treasured the promises of God about
us in their hearts (Luke 2:19),
presented us to the Lord as babies (Luke 2:22),
corrected us when we needed it (Luke 2:48),
and called out God's gifts in us (John 2:3-5).
You have modeled the grace-full life to us.

A Grace-Full Life: God's All-Reaching, Soul-Saving, Character-Shaping, Never-Ending Love Leader Guide

This book is printed on elemental chlorine-free paper.

ISBN 9781501832833

17 18 19 20 21 22 23 24 25 26 — 10 9 8 7 6 5 4 3 2 1
MANUFACTURED IN THE UNITED STATES OF AMERICA

Contents

About the Authors

Jorge Acevedo and **Wes Olds** are both pastors at Grace Church, a multisite United Methodist congregation in southwest Florida with six campuses. The church has grown in its weekend attendance from 400 to over 2,600 in the past nineteen years and has a remarkable ministry to, with, and for the poor, marginalized, and addicted. The church is recognized as having one of the largest and most effective recovery ministries in America.

Jorge is in his twenty-first year as the lead pastor at Grace Church and is the co-author of *Sent: Giving the Gift of Hope at Christmas, Vital: Churches Changing Communities and the World* and *The Heart of Youth Ministry.* Born in Puerto Rico, Jorge moved with his family at age four months to the United States where he was raised. Jorge and his wife, Cheryl, are the parents of two sons and have four grandchildren. Jorge's passion is to connect people to God and the church.

Wes is in his eleventh year as the campus pastor of the Cape Coral campus of Grace Church and is also a leadership coach with Spiritual Leadership, Inc. (SLI). Wes and his wife, Becky, have one teenage son, Caleb. Wes's passions are helping people discover they are "Children of God and Persons of Worth" and serving as a change agent for local churches to return to biblical Christianity in the Wesleyan way.

Jorge and Wes have a unique thirty-three-year friendship that began when Jorge was Wes's youth pastor through his high school years. Together they have served at three churches for more than fifteen years.

In *A Grace-Full Life,* Jorge and Wes share a Wesleyan understanding of grace in a very warm, personal style with strong life application. Their hope is that you will journey with them into a deeper understanding of God's amazing grace.

Introduction

Most of us grew up hearing messages from our parents, teachers, and other leaders that sounded right to us then, but that later in life we questioned. How many of us heard messages like these?

> Do your best!
> Work hard!
> If you want something done right, then do it yourself!

In and of themselves, these messages seem harmless and, frankly, can be helpful. There is nothing wrong with doing your best and working hard. But there is a danger when these childhood messages creep into our relationship with God.

These messages speak of our human efforts, abilities, and achievements, and are fine when applied to playing Little League or practicing the piano. But here's the danger: When we apply these messages of effort, ability, and achievement to our relationship with God, God becomes a cruel tyrant who wants us to do better, and we become beaten-down perfectionists who can never do enough to please and appease our cruel, divine Taskmaster.

That's why we're so grateful for grace. In fact, we aren't just grateful for grace; we're counting on grace! Grace is God's unconditional love for all of creation. It's the reality that there is nothing you can do to make God love you more, and there's nothing you can do to make God love you less. Grace means that all our efforts, abilities, and achievements can never make God love and accept us, but in the gift of amazing grace through God's Son Jesus, "God demonstrates his own love for us…while we were yet sinners" (Romans 5:8).

Through this study, your group will discover and discuss what it means to live a grace-full life. Over the next four weeks, you'll dive into each chapter and into the Scriptures to explore four aspects or seasons of God's grace, each of which can be described with a short phrase beginning with the word even:

Even There: God's All-Reaching Love
(Prevenient Grace)
Even Now: God's Soul-Saving Love
(Justifying Grace)
Even More: God's Character-Shaping Love
(Sanctifying Grace)
Even When: God's Never-Ending Love
(Glorifying Grace)

About the Study

Before the first session, you will want to distribute copies of the participant book to the members of your group. Be sure to communicate that they are to read the first chapter before your first group session.

As you gather each week with your group, you will have the opportunity to watch a video, discuss and respond to what you're learning, and pray together. You will need access to a television and DVD player with working remotes.

This leader guide and the DVD will be your primary tools for leading each group session. In this book you will find outlines for four group sessions, each formatted for a 60-minute session:

60-Minute Format

Leader Prep (Before the Session)	
Gathering	3 minutes
Warm Up	5 minutes
Video	12-14 minutes
Group Discussion	30-35 minutes
Closing Prayer	3-5 minutes

Feel free to adapt or modify the format in any way to meet the specific needs and preferences of your group. If you would like to extend the session to 90 minutes, simply increase the group discussion and prayer time. Here is a brief overview of the elements included:

Leader Prep (Before the Session)

This section provides an overview of the week's Scriptures and themes, a recap of the corresponding chapter, a list of materials and equipment needed, and some session goals. Be sure to read this section, as well as the session outline, before the session. You also may find it helpful to review the DVD segment in advance.

Gathering (3 minutes)

You may find that participants are rushed and distracted as they arrive (yourself included). Invite the group to settle in and open their hearts to what God might have for them during your time together. You may choose to read the written prayer provided for you or to pray an opening prayer of your own.

Warm Up (5 minutes)

Each session has a brief warm-up exercise to introduce the topic and set the tone for discussion.

Video (12-14 minutes)

Next, watch the week's video segment together.

Group Discussion (30-35 minutes)

After watching the video, use the discussion points and questions provided to facilitate group discussion. The discussion points are excerpts from the corresponding chapter of *A Grace-Full Life*. You may choose to read aloud the discussion points or express them in your own words. Use one or more of the questions that follow to guide your conversation.

Note that more discussion points and questions have been provided than you will have time to include. Beforehand, select those you want to cover, and put a check mark beside them. Reflect on each question and make some notes in the margins to share during your discussion time.

Rather than attempting to bulldoze through, be open to where the Spirit takes the conversation. Remember that your role is not to have all of the answers but to encourage discussion and sharing.

Closing Prayer (3-5 minutes)

Close by leading the group in prayer. Invite the group to name prayer requests. You might share a request of your own to get things started.

As the study progresses, encourage members to participate in the closing prayer by praying aloud for one another and the requests given. Make sure nametags are visible so that group members do not feel awkward if they do not remember someone's name.

After the prayer, remind the group to pray for one another throughout the week.

Before You Begin

As group leader, your role is to guide and encourage the group to fully participate in this study experience. Wherever they are in their faith journey, invite them to seek God, search the Scriptures, and expect an encounter with God's grace.

Leader Helps

- Pray for wisdom and discernment from the Holy Spirit, for you and for each member of the group, as you prepare for the study.
- Before each session, familiarize yourself with the content. Read the designated book chapter, and read through the session outline in this leader guide. You also may want to view the video in advance.
- Choose the session elements you will use during the group session, including the specific discussion questions you plan to cover. Be prepared, however, to adjust the session as group members interact and as questions arise. Prepare carefully, but allow space for the Holy Spirit to move in and through the group members and through you as facilitator.
- Prepare the space where the group will meet so that the space will enhance the learning process. Ideally, group members should be seated around a table or in a circle so

that all can see one another. Moveable chairs are best, so that the group easily can form pairs or small groups for discussion.

- Create a climate of openness where participants feel encouraged to contribute to the discussion. Remember that some people will jump right in with answers and ideas, while others will need time to process what is being discussed.
- If you notice that some participants seem never to be able to enter the conversation, ask them if they have thoughts to share. Give everyone a chance to talk, but keep the conversation moving. Moderate to prevent a few individuals from doing all the talking.
- Do not be afraid of silence. If no one speaks in response to a question, count silently to ten, then say something such as, "Would anyone like to go first?" If no one responds, offer an answer yourself and ask for comments.
- Model openness as you share with the group. Group members will follow your example. If you limit your sharing to a surface level, others will follow suit.
- Encourage multiple answers or responses before moving on to the next discussion topic.
- Ask, "Why?" or "Why do you believe that?" or "Can you say more about that?" to help continue the discussion and give it greater depth.
- Affirm others' responses with comments such as "Great" or "Thanks" or "Good insight"—especially if it's the first time someone has spoken during the group session.
- Monitor your own contributions. If you are doing most

of the talking, back off so that you do not train the group to listen rather than speak up.

- Remember that you do not have all the answers. Your job is to keep the discussion going and encourage participation.
- Honor the time schedule. If a session is running longer than expected, get consensus from the group before continuing beyond the agreed-upon ending time.
- Involve group members in various aspects of the group session, such as saying prayers or reading the Scripture.
- Note that the session guides sometimes call for breaking into smaller groups or pairs. This gives everyone a chance to speak and participate fully. Mix up the groups; don't let the same people group up for every activity.
- As always in discussions that may involve sharing personal information, confidentiality is essential. Participants should never pass along stories that have been shared in the group. Remind participants at each session that confidentiality is crucial to the success of this study.

Four Seasons of Grace

"Even There"

Prevenient Grace

Our lives, our very breath, is a gift of God's grace. God created the heavens and the earth, and God lovingly placed each of us in the midst of it all. The best description in the Bible of God's very essence and character is "God is love" (1 John 4:8), and God's love is unconditional. No matter where we go or what we do, God's grace is there. That is God's all-reaching, prevenient grace.

Psalm 139 tells us four things about the God who is drawing us into a relationship through prevenient grace:

1. *God knows everything about each of us.* God is working on our behalf even when we cannot see it or understand it. Because our lives are always in our all-knowing God's tender hands, we can choose to fill the gap with trust.

2. *God is everywhere we go.* Theologians call this God's omnipresence, which is God's capacity to be everywhere.

God is persistent, tireless, and lovingly resolved to convince us to recognize and respond to his grace. God's relentless tenderness works to awaken our souls to his invitation to come live in "the unforced rhythms of grace" (Matthew 11:28-30 *The Message*).

3. *God made each one of us.* Like a master craftsman, God shaped, formed, and fashioned every one of us. As the Apostle Paul wrote, "For we are his workmanship" (Ephesians 2:10a KJV). Each of us is God's masterpiece, created with amazing possibilities and tremendous potential.

4. *God can handle our "ugly."* In the middle of the raw stuff of our lives, God pursues us. The story of the Bible is God's gigantic search-and-rescue mission for humanity. Our "ugly" does not disqualify us from God's grace.

Our God is an "even there" God who is able to reach us no matter how far we have drifted away. God is always actively working to woo us to himself.

"Even Now"

Justifying Grace

The Bible often is described as a dynamic love story. In the New Testament, Jesus compares himself to a bridegroom longing to be with his bride. If the seasons of grace were to be compared to a couple's relationship, God's prevenient, "even there" grace would be the season of dating. It's the work God does before we say "yes" to God. God's soul-saving, justifying, "even now" grace is what makes us able to respond to God's proposal for a relationship that he has been pursuing with us since before we were even aware of it—all to hear us say "yes" to God's proposal of grace.

This "yes" can come in a moment or in a season of a person's life. Some people become followers of Jesus in what might be called a "light switch" experience. Think of the Apostle Paul's conversion on the Damascus Road (Acts 9). One moment the person is not a follower of Jesus. Then in an instant, like a light switch being flipped on, the Holy Spirit reaches them and they say "yes" to Jesus.

Others become followers of Jesus in a "dimmer switch" experience. A dimmer switch allows you to slowly increase the brightness of a light. When you click the knob on, the light is very dim. Then, as you turn the knob, the light shines brighter and brighter. A biblical example of a dimmer switch experience of grace is the bewildered disciples on the Emmaus Road who met the stranger, Jesus, as they walked with him. Confused because of Jesus' death on the cross, they wondered what their future held. Their witness was, "Didn't our hearts burn within us as he talked with us on the road?" (Luke 24:32). In the journey of walking and talking with Jesus, their hearts were warmed. It wasn't a moment. It was more like a season.

Whether God saves and justifies us in a moment or a season, God longs to be in a continually growing relationship with each of us. Long before we are aware of God's grace, God looks forward to the day or season in our lives when we will say "yes" to this proposal. God's saving grace is available "even now."

"Even More"

Sanctifying Grace

God loves us, and he wants to grow us up into the likeness of Jesus. This is God's character-shaping, sanctifying grace. God's grace not only provides a way to get to heaven *someday*; it also starts a lifelong adventure of letting God love us so that God can move more of heaven into our hearts *now*. That's sanctification—the "even more" of God's grace.

Salvation is much more than "fire insurance" against eternal separation from God or a holy evacuation plan to escape earth. Salvation is when our souls are restored to wholeness and health so that we are free to love God, receive God's abundant love into our lives, and then freely love others. Loving God, self, and others is what it means to be sanctified.

Experiencing God's justifying grace is just the beginning of the Christian life. The day of your salvation is like your "spiritual birthday." When you say "yes" to Jesus as your Savior, the conversion from old to new, from darkness to light, from death to life is a miracle that happens in a moment or a season. After that, there is a whole new life to grow into and live. Cooperating with God's sanctifying grace so that you are transformed into the image of Christ is an ongoing process.

Full life is found in loving God, letting God love us, and loving others. This is how we are to respond to God's character-shaping, sanctifying, "even more" grace; and it is a process that continues until the day we meet Jesus face-to-face.

"Even When"

Glorifying Grace

God loves us, and God's grace carries us from this life to the next. This is God's never-ending, glorifying grace that enables us to live and die well. John Wesley taught the early Methodists to live lives so that they could die "good deaths." A physician who treated several Methodists made this claim to Charles Wesley:

> *Most people die for fear of dying: but I never met with such people as yours. They are none of them afraid of death; but [are] calm, and patient, and resigned to the last.*[1]

1. The Journal of Charles Wesley, April 3–September 22, 1741. http://wesley.nnu.edu/charles-wesley/the-journal-of-charles-wesley-1707-1788/the-journal-of-charles-wesley-april-3-september-22-1741/. (The Wesley Center Online web site is a collection of historical and scholarly resources about the Wesleyan Tradition, theology, Christianity, and the Nazarene church. Copyright © 1993-2011. Wesley Center for Applied Theology, c/o Northwest Nazarene University. All Rights Reserved.) Accessed October 25, 2016.

John Wesley himself was a student of what was called "the art of dying." He and his people knew how to die well. We can be like them, learning to die well, in two simple, yet profound, ways:

1. *We can die well when we live confidently in Christ* ***now***. Dying well is a process that begins on this side of the veil of death as we live fully in Christ. The secret of dying well is living well with the assurance that because we belong to Jesus in this life, being with Jesus in the life to come will be even more glorious. When our lives belong to Christ, not even death scares us.

2. *We can die well when we know we will live completely in Christ* ***then***. The apostle Paul wrote, "[God] gives us victory over sin and death through our Lord Jesus Christ" (1 Corinthians 15:54-57). He lived with a courageous, deep-seated conviction that in Jesus' death, burial, and resurrection that death, hell, sin, and the grave had been defeated. Jesus' bold declaration "It is finished" resonated through Paul's soul in this life so that he lived assured of life eternal. Whether death comes to you slowly or quickly, whether it comes late in life or way too early, the Bible teaches us that if we are followers of Jesus, we do not need to fear death.

God's "even there," prevenient grace woos us to Jesus. God's "even now," justifying grace saves us. God's "even more," sanctifying grace transforms us into the image of Christ. And God's "even when," glorifying grace welcomes us into eternity.

Session Outlines

Session 1

Even There

God's All-Reaching Love

(Prevenient Grace)

I can never escape from your Spirit!
I can never get away from your presence!
If I go up to heaven, you are there;
if I go down to the grave, you are there.
If I ride the wings of the morning,
if I dwell by the farthest oceans,
even there your hand will guide me,
and your strength will support me.

(Psalm 139:7-10)

Leader Prep

Session Goals

Through this session's discussion, participants will:

- Explore the concept of prevenient grace;
- Discover the ways God has been seeking them;
- Receive the truth that God knows, is everywhere we go, made us unique, and can handle all of our ugly;
- Be real before God and receive God's grace.

Preparation

- Read the first chapter, "Even There: God's All-Reaching Love: Prevenient Grace," in *A Grace-Full Life* by Jorge Acevedo and Wes Olds.
    - o Read through this session outline in its entirety to familiarize yourself with the material being covered.
    - o Read and reflect on the following Scriptures: 1 Samuel 16:7; Psalm 8:3-4; Psalm 139; Isaiah 59:1; Matthew 6:25-30.
    - o Have a markerboard or large sheet of paper available for recording group members' ideas.
    - o Have a Bible, paper for taking notes, and a pen or pencil available for every participant.

What You Will Need

- *A Grace-Full Life* DVD and DVD player
- Stick-on nametags and markers (if needed)
- Slips of paper and pens
- Extra Bibles

Session Outline

Gathering (3 minutes)

Hand out nametags and markers, and ask participants to write their names and wear the nametags for the session. Welcome the participants and remind them that you will be spending the next four weeks exploring a life of grace. When you are ready to begin the session, pray the opening prayer below or a prayer of your own.

God of Grace, we thank you for your incredible, unbelievable grace that seems too good to be true! Thank you for knowing us, for being with us, and for loving us so much that you can handle every bit of who we are. Open our eyes to see what it looks like to live a grace-full life. May we grow closer to you and to one another as we study your Word. Amen.

Warm Up (5 minutes)

Hand out slips of paper and pens. Ask participants to write on their slips a definition of prevenient grace. They can write an actual attempt at a definition, if they are familiar with the concept, or can make up something. Place all the papers in a basket. Then, read aloud some of them and ask for comments on the definitions. (You might have participants rate each definition on a scale of one to five, based on how accurate they think each definition is.) After reading aloud the definitions, tell participants that prevenient grace is the "even there" grace with which God seeks us, woos us, and draws us to God—and that's what you'll be exploring in today's discussion.

Video (12-14 minutes)

Play the Week 1 video segment on the DVD.

Group Discussion (30-35 minutes)

More discussion points and questions have been provided than you will have time to include. Beforehand, select those you want to cover, and place a check mark beside them. Page numbers from the study book are provided for reference.

1. David's stargazing caused him to soul-gaze and consider an amazing reality that many of us are either unaware of or too busy to ponder. (See Psalm 8:3-4.) The God who put the stars in outer space and put our sun and moon in place cares for you and me. We call God's constant love and care for us grace. Grace is the reality that the Creator of the universe deeply cares for and loves each and every one of us (page 23).
    - Read aloud Psalm 8:3-4. What, do you think, was David feeling when he wrote these words?
    - When have you been lost in wonder that the Creator of the universe knows you by name?

2. We have a God who is like a daddy anxious to care for the needs of his children. Jesus tells us to "look up" at the birds of the air and "look out" at the flowers of the fields. These are living witnesses to the gentle care and tender love of God. These are nature's testimonies of God's grace for you and me (page 24).
    - Read Matthew 6:25-30. What is Jesus talking about when he compares us to birds and flowers?
    - When or why is it difficult for you to believe that God will take care of you?

- o Would you say that you live your life as though you believe that God is good and will care for you? Why, or why not?

3. Your life—your very breath—is a gift of God's grace. God created the heavens and the earth, and God lovingly placed you in the midst of it all (page 24).
   - o Read aloud 1 John 4:8. What does this verse say about God?
   - o What does it mean that God is love?
   - o How would your life be different if you lived out a belief that all of life is a gift of grace?

4. The good news of Jesus is that we don't have to climb our way into heaven. Heaven has come to us. God is a missionary God who is on an all-out search-and-rescue mission for all people everywhere and in every time who are made in God's image (page 48-49).
   - o Read Luke 19:1-10. Who was Jesus on a mission to reach?
   - o When have you experienced feeling like God was on a mission to reach you?
   - o How have you been a part of God's missionary work to reach others?

5. Every person on this planet is crazy about Jesus. They just don't know it yet! So, God is on an all-out search for us. That is prevenient grace. God is "even there" when we don't know it or expect it (page 24).
   - o What is your reaction to the statement that every person on the planet is crazy about Jesus but just doesn't know it yet?

- o When did you discover that Jesus is crazy about you?
- o How does your life tell others that you are crazy about Jesus?

6. God has the capacity to look past the externals and into the core of who we really are. Theologians call this God's omniscience, which is God's capacity to know everything that there is to know. Some might see this as frightening, but David, in the Psalms, saw it as comforting (page 26).
   - o Read aloud Psalm 139:1-4. Do you hear anxiety or comfort in these words from David?
   - o How does it feel knowing that God knows each of us well and has eyes on us wherever we are?
   - o How does God's knowledge of you give you a sense of security?

7. David declares that neither the heights of heaven nor the depths of hell are beyond God's reach. This echoes the prophet Isaiah, who said, "Surely the arm of the Lord is not too short to save" (Isaiah 59:1a). Theologians call this God's omnipresence, which is God's capacity to be everywhere. God is persistent, tireless, and lovingly resolved to convince us to recognize and respond to God's grace (page 29, 31).
   - o Read aloud Psalm 139:5-12. What is David saying about God's knowledge of him?
   - o Have you ever tried to "outrun" God? How did you discover that you can't?

8. Like a master craftsman, God shaped, formed, and fashioned every one of us. As the Apostle Paul wrote, "We are his workmanship" (Ephesians 2:10a KJV). God made you, and that's why God is on an all-out search for you! (page 32).
    - o Read Psalm 139:13-18. How does knowing that God made each of us with purpose and creativity affect how you live and approach life?
    - o What do these verses say about the love and affection God has for us?

9. God is not afraid of our "ugly." In the middle of the raw stuff of our lives, God pursues us. The story of the Bible is God's gigantic search-and-rescue mission for humanity (page 34).
    - o Read Psalm 139:19-22. When have you experienced feelings similar to those David conveys in these verses?
    - o Read Romans 8:38-39. What level of "ugly" is too much for God to love you?
    - o Read Psalm 139:23-24. Where does David end up after discovering that God knows everything about him, made him uniquely, and sees him wherever he is?

10. Wrap up group discussion with these questions:
    - o What stood out to you in your study this week?
    - o What new insight did you gain about what it means to live a grace-full life?

Closing Prayer (3-5 minutes)

Close the session by taking prayer requests from participants and leading the group in prayer. As you progress to later weeks in the study, encourage members to participate in the closing prayer by praying aloud for each other and the requests given. Remind participants to pray for one another throughout the week.

Session 2

Even Now

God's Soul-Saving Love

(Justifying Grace)

As God's partners, we beg you not to accept this marvelous gift of God's kindness and then ignore it. For God says,

> *"At just the right time, I heard you.*
> *On the day of salvation, I helped you."*

Indeed, the "right time" is now. Today is the day of salvation.

(2 Corinthians 6:1-2)

Leader Prep

Session Goals

Through this session's discussion, participants will:

- Explore the concept of justifying grace;
- Learn or remember that all have sinned and fallen short of God's glory;
- Receive the truth that God calls our names and wants to be our friend;
- Be real before God and receive God's grace.

Preparation

- Read Chapter 2, "Even Now: God's Soul-Saving Love: Justifying Grace," in *A Grace-Full Life* by Jorge Acevedo and Wes Olds.
    - Read through this session outline in its entirety to familiarize yourself with the material being covered.
    - Read and reflect on the following Scriptures: Luke 19:1-9; Romans 2:23; 8:1; 2 Corinthians 6:1-2.
    - Have a markerboard or large sheet of paper available for recording participants' ideas.
    - Have a Bible, paper for taking notes, and a pen or pencil available for every participant.

What You Will Need

- *A Grace-Full Life* DVD and DVD player
- Stick-on nametags and markers (if needed)
- Extra Bibles

Session Outline

Gathering (3 minutes)

Hand out the nametags and markers, and ask participants to write their names and wear the nametags for the session. When it is time to begin, pray the opening prayer below or a prayer of your own.

God of Grace, we thank you for your saving grace! Thank you for seeking us out, knowing that we will fall short, and loving us even still. Teach us what it means to live a grace-full life. May we grow closer to you and to one another as we study your Word. Amen.

Warm Up (5 minutes)

Tell the group your conversion story. You may have had a life-changing, mountain-top experience that brought you into a relationship with Christ, or you may have grown into your faith slowly over the course of your life. Regardless, talk about how and why you are a Christian and when or how you felt the assurance of God's grace. Or if you prefer, invite a group member in advance to share his or her conversion story.

Then ask participants to think about their own stories. Remind them that there isn't a "right way" to come to Jesus, that he forgives and calls us friends whenever and wherever we find him.

Video (12-14 minutes)

Play the Week 2 video segment on the DVD.

Group Discussion (30-35 minutes)

More discussion points and questions have been provided than you will have time to include. Before the session, select those you want to cover, and put a check mark beside them. Page numbers from the study book are provided for reference.

1. If the seasons of grace were to be compared to a couple's relationship, God's prevenient, "even there" grace would be the season of dating. It's the work God does before we say "yes" to God. God's soul-saving, justifying, "even now" grace allows us to respond to God's proposal for a relationship that God has been pursuing with us since before we were even aware of it (page 43).
    - How has God pursued you?
    - What experiences of God have made you want to say, "Yes," to a relationship with God?
    - How have you answered God's "proposal"?

2. Some people become followers of Jesus in what we call a "light switch" experience. One moment the person is not a follower of Jesus. Then in an instant, like a light switch being flipped on, the Holy Spirit reaches that person and he or she says, "Yes," to Jesus. Others become followers of Jesus in a "dimmer switch" experience. A dimmer switch allows you to slowly increase the brightness of a light. When you click the knob on, the light is very dim. Then, as you turn the knob, the light shines brighter and brighter (page 43, 45).
    - Read aloud Acts 9:1-31. Describe the Apostle Paul's conversion experience.
    - Read Luke 24:13-35. How was the disciples' awareness of the risen Christ like a dimmer switch?

- o Would you describe your conversion as more of a light switch or dimmer switch? Why?
- o Why, do you think, do people respond to God's "even there" grace in different ways?

3. There have been times when we both have started to subtly believe and live a lie that says we can "get our salvation" the old-fashioned way—by earning it! Many people, intentionally or unintentionally, trust in a "performance plan" approach to finding salvation and lasting peace (page 46-47).
   - o When have you acted as though you had to earn your salvation and work your way into God's favor?
   - o Read about the "goodness scale" on page 47. Why, do you think, do we sometimes judge our goodness against others?
   - o Read Romans 2:23. How does Paul feel about a "goodness scale"? Who, according to Paul, would pass the goodness test?

4. God desires our friendship. Together friends can think through problems and situations and make better judgments than they would individually. Friends usually bring out better versions of each other because people behave better when they know their friends are observing (page 50).
   - o Read Luke 19:1-10. What can we assume about the number of friends Zacchaeus had?
   - o What is significant about Jesus noticing Zacchaeus in the tree and calling him by name?
   - o How did Jesus express to Zacchaeus that he wanted to be his friend?

- o How has Jesus reached out to you in friendship?
- o How has Jesus been a friend to you?

5. God offers us forgiveness. The good news of God's love through Jesus is that God's grace finds us—even now! What happens when we say "yes" to Jesus as our Savior is that our position before God changes. When we accept the gift of forgiveness of our sins, we become "justified." That means that—when God looks at you and me, covered by the blood of Jesus that has the power to wash away sin—God does not see our sin (page 56).
    - o Why was the crowd annoyed that Jesus wanted to spend time with Zacchaeus?
    - o Maybe, on the goodness scale, we aren't complete scoundrels like Zacchaeus, but why do we nonetheless need God's forgiveness?
    - o How have you known the power of God's forgiveness in your life or seen it at work in someone else's life?

6. God wants to give us a future. Short on friends and short on forgiveness, Zacchaeus was also short on a future. He had no sense of purpose or destiny except to grow richer and become more and more lost in his loneliness, shame, and sense of meaninglessness. This one encounter with Jesus changed all of that. Having been welcomed by God as Jesus entered his home and life, Zacchaeus experienced new life. His empty soul was filled with purpose. (page 58).
    - o How did Jesus give Zacchaeus a sense of purpose and a future?

- o God rewrote Zacchaeus's story; how has God been rewriting yours?

7. The notion of God's love coming to us free of charge, no strings attached, seems to go against our every instinct. Most worldviews, whether religious or secular, offer ways for us to earn approval and find forgiveness. Only Jesus dares to make God's love unconditional by taking it upon himself to atone for our sins. When we realize this, understanding that we don't have to strive to win God's favor or earn God's grace, we truly have reason to celebrate (page 60-61)!
   - o Why is God's no-strings-attached love such a difficult concept for us?
   - o Why is God's grace a reason to celebrate?
   - o How has God's grace changed your life?

8. Wrap up group discussion with these questions:
   - o What stood out to you in your study this week?
   - o What new insight did you gain about what it means to live a grace-full life?

Closing Prayer (3-5 minutes)

Close the session by taking prayer requests from participants and leading the group in prayer. Encourage members to participate in the closing prayer by praying aloud for each other and the requests given. Remind participants to pray for one another throughout the week.

Session 3

Even More

God's Character-Shaping Love

(Sanctifying Grace)

My response is to get down on my knees before the Father, this magnificent Father who parcels out all heaven and earth. I ask him to strengthen you by his Spirit—not a brute strength but a glorious inner strength—that Christ will live in you as you open the door and invite him in. And I ask him that with both feet planted firmly on love, you'll be able to take in with all followers of Jesus the extravagant dimensions of Christ's love. Reach out and experience the breadth! Test its length! Plumb the depths! Rise to the heights! Live full lives, full in the fullness of God.

(*Ephesians 3:14-19* The Message)

Leader Prep

Session Goals

Through this session's discussion, participants will be encouraged to:

- Explore the concept of sanctifying grace;
- Discover that God's ongoing, sanctifying grace continually transforms us;
- Receive the truth that God never runs out of grace for us;
- Be real before God and receive God's grace.

Preparation

- Read Chapter 3, "Even More: God's Character-Shaping Love: Sanctifying Grace," in *A Grace-Full Life* by Jorge Acevedo and Wes Olds.
    - Read through this session outline in its entirety to familiarize yourself with the material being covered.
    - Read and reflect on the following Scriptures: Romans 7:18-20; 8:1-2; Ephesians 3:14-21; 4:1-6; Philippians 3:10-11. Have a markerboard or large sheet of paper available for recording participants' ideas.
    - Have a Bible, paper for taking notes, index cards, and a pen or pencil available for every participant.

What You Will Need

- *A Grace-Full Life* DVD and DVD player
- Stick-on nametags and markers (if needed)
- Extra Bibles

Session Outline

Gathering (3 minutes)

Hand out the nametags and markers, and ask participants to write their names and wear the nametags for the session. When it is time to begin, pray the opening prayer below or a prayer of your own.

God of Grace, we thank you for your sanctifying grace! Thank you for seeking us out, knowing that we will fall short, loving us even still, and transforming us into Jesus' likeness. Teach us what it means to live a grace-full life. May we grow closer to you and to one another as we study your Word. Amen.

Warm Up (5 minutes)

Remind participants of the "Wait . . . there's more" commercial analogy found on page 66. Hand out index cards and pens or pencils. Ask participants, in pairs or groups of three, to write an infomercial-style pitch for God's sanctifying grace. On one side of the card, have groups write a definition of sanctifying grace in their own words; on the other side of the card have them list some "But wait! There's more" bullet points that describe what kind of changes God's grace can make in our lives. After a few minutes, ask pairs and groups to read what they've written.

Video (12-14 minutes)

Play the Week 3 video segment on the DVD.

Group Discussion (30-35 minutes)

More discussion points and questions have been provided than you will have time to include. Before the session, select those you want to cover, and put a check mark beside them. Page numbers from the study book are provided for reference.

1. God's grace not only provides a way to get to heaven someday; grace also starts a lifelong adventure of letting God love us so that God's kingdom can be at work in our hearts and lives now. That's sanctification—the "even more" of God's grace (page 66).
   - How important to your faith is being with God in heaven in the future?
   - How important to your faith is an ongoing, life-changing walk with God?
   - When has looking ahead to the future kept you from understanding or appreciating what God was doing in your life at the moment?
   - How can God's grace change us?
   - When have you experienced an "even-more" kind of grace?

2. While Christians sometimes act as though salvation is just "fire insurance" against eternal separation from God or a holy evacuation plan to one day escape earth, salvation is much more. Salvation is when our souls are restored to wholeness and health so that we are free to love God, receive God's abundant love into our lives, and freely love others. Saying "yes" to Jesus as our Savior—the conversion from old to new, from darkness to light, from death to life—is a miracle that happens in a moment or a season. But cooperating with God's grace

so that we are transformed into the image of Christ takes a lifetime (page 67).

- o What does it mean to think of salvation as "fire insurance"? Why is this view of salvation shortsighted?
- o How has God's grace made it possible for you to love God, yourself, and your neighbor?
- o What does it mean to be transformed into the image of Christ?
- o In what ways is God transforming you into a reflection of Christ?

3. Through Jesus' work on the cross and the tomb, we have been freed from judgment and sin's insidious grip. Yet all of us still wrestle with sin. We must live in the tension between our position in Christ (what Christ says about us) and our condition in Christ (how we are in "real time" walking with Christ). Sanctification is the journey to close the gap between our position and our condition in Christ (page 68-69).
   - o Read aloud Romans 8:1-2 and Romans 7:18-20. What tension is in play in these two Scripture verses from Paul's letter?
   - o When have you felt as though your position in Christ and your condition in Christ were in conflict? How did you work through this conflict?
   - o How do these verses from Romans help you consider what it looks like to live a life in grace?

4. The goal of grace is not to have a one-time experience of accepting Christ. God's "even more," sanctifying grace

is a lifelong relationship. The goal of grace is that we would love God more and more (page 71).

- o Read Philippians 3:10. Who and what is Paul seeking?
- o How is our relationship with God like a marriage relationship?
- o What does it take to love God more?

5. Knowing and loving God more takes time. Just as our relationships with people we love require meaningful time, so does our relationship with God (page 72).
   - o Refer to page 73 in *A Grace-Full Life*. What is the SOAP method? How can this tool help you deepen your relationship with God through reading Scripture?
   - o What, would you say, is the current state of your relationship with God? Daily encounters? Every-now-and-then? A memory from your younger years?
   - o What do you want your relationship with God to look like?

6. Another way we can experience and respond to God's sanctifying, "even more" grace is through healing. Jesus wants to save us from separation from God not only eternally but also here and now. God's "even more" sanctifying grace makes this second part a reality. We can think of Jesus' ministry as threefold: preaching (declaring the Kingdom), teaching (explaining the Kingdom), and healing (demonstrating the Kingdom). Jesus' healing ministry was his ministry that healed broken bodies, calmed emotional distress, cast out demons, and even raised the dead (page 74-75).

- o What do you know about Jesus' ministry of healing?
- o In what ways is Jesus still in the ministry of healing today?
- o How have you known the power of Jesus' healing in your life?

7. God put on a disguise by taking on the form of a man named Jesus and coming into our messy, ordinary lives. When Jesus reveals himself as our Savior, forgiving all our sins by his own blood, overcoming death so we never have to die, and positioning and presenting us to God the Father as perfect, what are we to do? Our "work" in response to this amazing grace is to love others even more (page 77).
    - o Read Ephesians 4:1-6. What does Paul teach us to do in response to God's amazing grace?
    - o Who are the people in your sphere of influence who are desperate to know God's love and grace? How can you give them a glimpse of what God offers them?

8. A famous anonymous quotation (often mistakenly attributed to Mark Twain) says, "The two most important days in your life are the day you are born and the day you find out why." To love God and love others as we love ourselves is why you and I were created. Life is more than waiting to get to heaven. Full life is found in loving God, embracing God's love of us, and loving others. This is how we are to respond to God's character-shaping, sanctifying, "even more" grace; and it is a process that continues until the day we meet Jesus face-to-face (page 79-80).

- o What have you discovered about why you were created?
- o How are you living your life as a response to God's amazing grace?

9. Wrap up group discussion with these questions:
   - o What stood out to you in your study this week?
   - o What new insight did you gain about what it means to live a grace-full life?

Closing Prayer (3-5 minutes)

Close the session by taking prayer requests from participants and leading the group in prayer. Encourage members to participate in the closing prayer by praying aloud for each other and the requests given. Remind participants to pray for one another throughout the week.

Session 4

Even When

God's Never-Ending Love

(Glorifying Grace)

And I am convinced that nothing can ever separate us from God's love. Neither death nor life, neither angels nor demons, neither our fears for today nor our worries about tomorrow—not even the powers of hell can separate us from God's love. No power in the sky above or in the earth below—indeed, nothing in all creation will ever be able to separate us from the love of God that is revealed in Christ Jesus our Lord.

(Romans 8:38-39)

Leader Prep

Session Goals

Through this session's discussion, participants will:

- Explore the concept of glorifying grace;
- Discover that God has a glorifying grace that gifts us with the ability to die well;
- Receive the truth that God promises that there is no fear in death;
- Be real before God and receive God's grace.

Preparation

- Read Chapter 4, "Even When: God's Never-Ending Love: Glorifying Grace," in *A Grace-Full Life* by Jorge Acevedo and Wes Olds.
    - o Read through this session outline in its entirety to familiarize yourself with the material being covered.
    - o Read and reflect on the following Scriptures: Matthew 20:1-15; Luke 15:11-32; 23:39-43; Romans 8:38-39; 1 Corinthians 15:54-57; Philippians 1:21; 2 Timothy 4:6-7; 1 John 4:18; Revelation 3:20.
    - o Have a markerboard or large sheet of paper available for recording participants' ideas.
    - o Have a Bible, paper for taking notes, and a pen or pencil available for every participant.

What You Will Need

- *A Grace-Full Life* DVD and DVD player
- Stick-on nametags and markers (if needed)
- Extra Bibles

Session Outline

Gathering (3 minutes)

Hand out the nametags and markers, and ask participants to write their names and wear the nametags for the session. When it is time to begin, pray the opening prayer below or a prayer of your own.

God of grace and glory, we thank you for your glorifying grace! Thank you that we truly have no fear in death. Teach us what it means to live a grace-full life. May we grow closer to you and to one another as we study your Word. Amen.

Warm Up (5 minutes)

Hand out index cards and pens. Ask participants to write an epitaph (a sentence or two honoring a deceased person, usually placed on a tombstone) for themselves, imagining how they want to be remembered. After a few minutes, invite volunteers to read aloud their epitaphs.

Video (12-14 minutes)

Play the Week 4 video segment on the DVD.

Group Discussion (30-35 minutes)

More discussion points and questions have been provided than you will have time to include. Before the session, select those you want to cover, and place a check mark beside them. Page numbers from the study book are provided for reference.

1. Do you recall the story of Ed, who at almost the very same moment he was saying, "Goodbye! I'll see you later!" to one of his church's dying saints was also receiving notice that he would be saying, "Hello! Welcome to this world!" to his first grandchild? (Direct participants to page 81.) This is a picture of the life of grace from the cradle to the grave, from the womb to the tomb, from the first breath to the last. This is the scope and scale of God's grace. Living in this grace, our life is secure (pages 81-82).
   - Why is our life in God's grace described as "secure"?
   - Read aloud Romans 8:38-39 and 1 John 4:18. How do these verses establish your feeling of security?
   - How secure do you feel about death and dying? Why?

2. John Wesley, an eighteenth-century pastor in the Church of England, began a movement among a group of his friends that spread throughout England and North America. His movement, Methodism, took off after Wesley had an experience that assured him of his salvation and relieved him of his fear of death. This is the gift of God's "even when," glorifying grace. This is God's never-ending love for us that enables us to live and die well (page 82-84).
   - Read the excerpt from John Wesley's journal on page 84. What, do you think, did he mean when he described his heart feeling "strangely warmed"?

- o Have you ever had a "heart-strangely-warmed" encounter with God?
- o What assures you that God has delivered you from your sins and that you can look forward to an eternal future with God?

3. As followers of Christ, we all want to die well. John Wesley taught that we should live life in a way that we might die "good deaths" (page 85).
   - o What does it mean to die a "good death"?
   - o How does the way we live our lives affect how we die?
   - o Read 2 Timothy 4:6-7. What does this Scripture tell us about living a life that leads to a good death?
   - o In what ways are you currently fighting the good fight and running your race?

4. Our culture glamorizes youth and beauty and denies the reality that the mortality rate still hovers right at 100 percent! Hear this truth from Paul: The key to dying well is living well! Paul lived well. His put his whole life into fighting the good fight and finishing the race. He was faithful to God. He lived well (page 86).
   - o Read aloud Philippians 1:21. What does Paul mean by this?
   - o What does your life look like when you live according to this verse?
   - o What is gained in death?

5. Paul's confidence was secure because he knew that, whether he lived or died, he belonged to Jesus. That gave him great confidence in living. Because he belonged to

Jesus in this life, he believed that being with Jesus in the life to come would be even more glorious. That's living well. When our lives belong to Christ on this side of the veil of death, not even death scares us (page 87).

- o Do you think people are generally afraid of dying? Explain.
- o What does our culture say about death?
- o What do Christians have to say to the world about death?

6. [We can] live confidently in Christ now [when we] cultivate holy living. This requires intentional self-examination (page 89).
   - o What do you want the most important people in your life to say about you at your funeral?
   - o How does your answer to this question affect the way you live your life?

7. Please do not misunderstand us to say that if you live confidently in Christ before death, you are promised a "Hallmark moment" death with your family praying and singing hymns around you. That may happen.
   But sometimes death comes as a surprising, unwelcomed visitor that even may bring physical pain and relational heartache. A heart attack or car accident can quickly and tragically steal a life away. Whether death comes to you slowly or quickly, whether it comes late in life or way too early, the Bible teaches us that if you are a follower of Jesus, you do not need to fear death (page 93).
   - o Read 1 Corinthians 15:54-58. What is Paul teaching us about our deaths?

- o Read Revelation 3:20. What is promised in this verse?

8. [Parables] are not simply stories about the nature and character of God; they also are about the nature, character, and calling of followers of Jesus. We are called to extend God's unconditional love to a world that is lost, broken, and hurting. The God of the universe—Father, Son and Holy Spirit—so graciously, generously, and quite unfairly extends grace to us (page 105-106).
   - o How has God softened your heart and given you more grace over the course of these sessions?
   - o What does it mean to extend grace to others?
   - o Read Matthew 20:1-15; Luke 15:11-32; 23:39-43. What is Jesus teaching us about grace? Can you imagine demonstrating this kind of grace? What can we do to increase our ability to extend grace freely?

9. Wrap up group discussion with these questions:
   - o What stood out to you in your study this week?
   - o What new insight did you gain about what it means to live a grace-full life?
   - o What is one of your primary takeaways from this study?

Closing Prayer (3-5 minutes)

Close the session by taking prayer requests from participants and leading the group in prayer. After giving thanks for all that God has taught you through this study, encourage members to participate in the closing prayer by praying aloud for each other and the requests given. Remind participants to continue praying for one another in the weeks to come.

CPSIA information can be obtained
at www.ICGtesting.com
Printed in the USA
LVOW01s0241260417
532027LV00004BA/8/P

9 781501 832833